Smells Good!

Julie Haydon

Contents

Rigby®

A Harcourt Achieve Imprint

www.Rigby.com

1-800-531-5015

Good Smells

This is my nose.

I smell things with my nose.

Some things smell good.

Some things smell bad.

Gran grows **herbs**
in her garden.
Some of the herbs
smell good.

Gran's Herb Bags

Gran makes herb bags.

She cuts some herbs.

She hangs them up to dry.

She puts the herbs

inside little bags.

Herb bags smell good.
I want an herb bag
for my room.
Gran will help me
make an herb bag.

What I Need

To make my herb bag,

I need:

- cloth

- scissors

- stuffing

- a spoon

- dry herbs that smell good

- a rubber band

- a ribbon

Cloth

My cloth is blue
on the outside
and white on the inside.

outside

inside

Gran helps me cut the cloth.

She cuts it into a square.

Stuffing

I put the stuffing
on the inside of the cloth.
The stuffing will make
the bag round.
We will not see
the stuffing.

Dry Herbs

I put some dry herbs on a spoon.

The herbs smell good.

I put the herbs on the cloth and on the stuffing.

My Herb Bag

I put the ends of the cloth over the herbs and stuffing. Gran helps me.

Gran helps me to put
a rubber band
around the cloth.
Then we put a ribbon
on the bag.

I put the herb bag
in my room.

I like my herb bag.

Now my room

will smell good!

Glossary

herbs